English interpretation by Karen Weller-Watson and Linnea Dayton
Calligraphy by Lusana Erekson
Art Direction for English version by Ed Roxburgh

ISBN O-915391-14-7
Library of Congress Catalog Card Number 85-61801

 An Avant Book™ copublished by:

Slawson Communications, Inc.   Oak Tree Publications
San Diego, California 92103-4316   San Diego, California 92123

THE PICTURE BOOK OF
Cats
Yoko Imoto

Waiting for kittens.

The kittens are here!

OUT FOR A STROLL.

Romp and play.

POUNCE AND ROLL.

Lick, Lick...smooth and clean.

Comfy, cozy.

PURR...

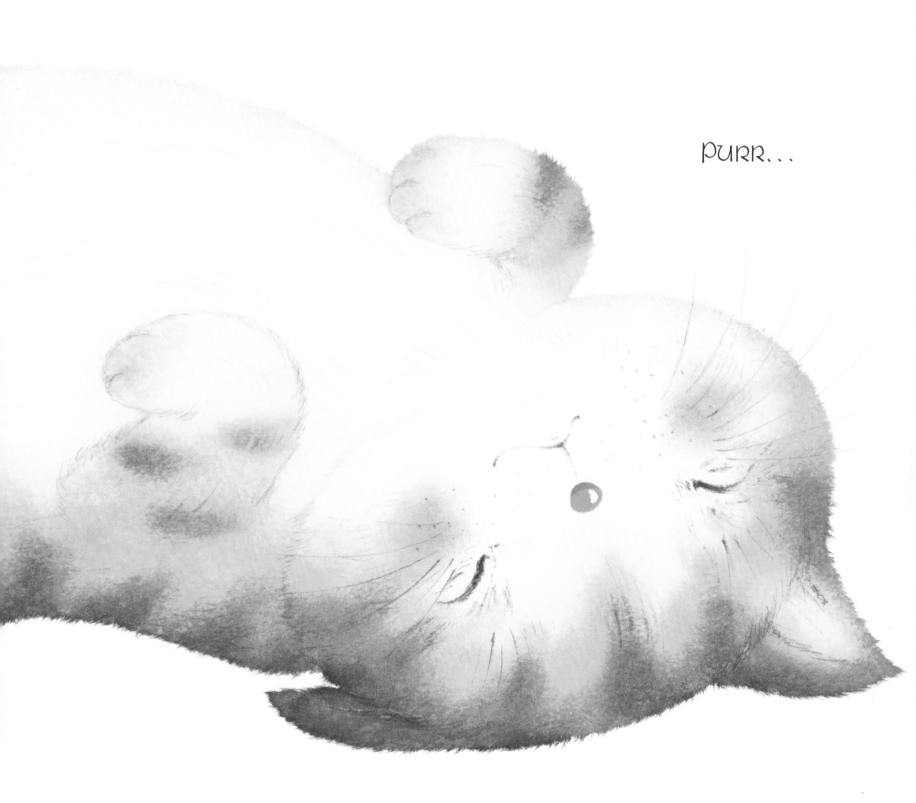

and dream.

Another cat family.

playing...

FiERCE!

Snuggling, and then...

Cleaning and smoothing.

Nap Time again.